D1215729

# Neal Bowers

# THE GOLF BALL DIVER

Neal Bowers

*Neal Bowers*

# THE GOLF BALL DIVER

## Prints by Michelle Anderson

Minnesota Voices Project #18

New Rivers Press 1983

Many of the poems in *The Golf Ball Diver* have been previously published
(some in slightly different versions) in the following periodicals: *American
Poetry Review*, *Ball State Forum*, *Chariton Review*, *Cimarron Review*,
*Great River Review*, *Greenfield Review*, *Hiram Poetry Review*, *Kansas
Quarterly*, *Louisville Review*, *New Letters*, *Panhandler*, *Pawn Review*,
*Poetry Northwest*, *Seattle Review*, *Southern Humanities Review*, *Southern
Poetry Review*, *and Sou'wester.* We wish to thank the editors of these
publications for permission to reprint in this volume. The author also wishes
to thank Ms. Daren Sinsheimer for her invaluable editorial assistance.

*The Golf Ball Diver* has been published with the aid of grants from the Iowa
State Research Foundation, the Iowa State University Graduate College, the
National Endowment for the Arts (with funds appropriated by the Congress
of the United States), and the Arts Development Fund of the United Arts
Council

New Rivers Press books are distributed by:

Bookslinger                and     Small Press Distribution, Inc.
213 East 4th St.                   1784 Shattuck Ave.
St. Paul, MN 55101                 Berkeley, CA 94709

*The Golf Ball Diver* has been manufactured in the United States of America
for New Rivers Press, Inc. (C. W. Truesdale, editor/publisher), 1602 Selby
Ave., St. Paul, MN 55104 in a first edition of 750 copies.

To the memory of my father
Floyd E. Bowers
1913-1979

# The Golf Ball Diver

## I

The Golf Ball Diver, 11
Floaters, 13
Foul Play, 14
Your Responsibility, 15
Diagnosis, 16
Elegy for a Writer in Residence, 17
Writer's Block, 18
Edges, 19
The Washday Ascension, 21
After the Flood, 22
Jigsaw Lovers, 24
Motherload, 25
The Sentry, 26
Saying, 27
Inheritance, 29
Farmer, 30
My Father's Best Picture, 31
The Passenger, 32

## II

Baking, 35
Caring for Succulents, 36
Naming the Icebergs, 37
Breakage, 38
Museo del Oro, Bogatá, 39
The One, 40
Rehearsal Dinner, 41
The Truth About the Universe, 42
Snow Ordinance, 44
Classified, 45
At the Railroad Crossing: A Practical Guide, 46
Endings, 47
The Haunting, 48
Waking as if from Sleep, 50

III

Clearing the Field, 53
Hunter's Moon, 54
Killing Weather, 55
The Sacrifice, 56
Tracker, 57
To My Unborn Children, 58
The Young Man Writes of Death, 60
To My Left Hand, 62
Sketching Audubon, 63
What Dying Must Be Like, 64
Pallbearers, 65
Lovely to Think So, 66
Notes, 67
Forty, 68
Making It Last, 69
The Secret, 70
Driving without Lights, 72

I

# The Golf Ball Diver

When the golf ball diver comes to town
with his wet suit draped across the back seat
like a spare life, the boys at the Skelly station
spread the word and half the population
shows up at the country club just in time
to see him slip into the water hazard,
the way something once stepped into a thicket
at the side of the road beyond the headlights
of the sherrif's car and a dog in a nearby yard
set up a howl so mournful and so long
the neighbors spent most of the night searching,
cursing sawbriars and mosquitoes.

What they found was how darkness curved back on itself,
kept them walking in circles, each man pacing
the inside circumference of his own black bin.
In the morning they laughed to see
how the trampled weeds lay like fairy rings,
but they brought nothing with them out of that field,
just a few chiggers and beggar lice
and a dew heavy in their clothes.

Now they wait with others on the fairway above
the pond strewn with algae and frog spawn,
watching the diver's bubbles, conjuring
things lost years ago—a hat left on the hook
in a Kansas cafe, remembered in Iowa, too late
to turn around; a ring missed at Kentucky Lake;
three forks gone without a clue from the silverware tray;
keys dropped through a corner grate; a letter,
used to make the page, left in a library book—
so many regrets, so many unsolved mysteries.

For thirty cents a ball, the diver will grope
all afternoon amid beer cans and bottles,
golf gloves waving like tentacles
in the thin light on the bottom,
and each time he surfaces the gallery
will whistle and applaud, happy
to have even this much returned.

# Floaters

*Another body, that of an apparent suicide, was
found floating today in the East River. Authorities
say the victim, submerged for several months, is
one of three to appear thus far during the recent
mild weather. —UPI*

They rise
on the first warm day in spring
as careless as flowers,
opening out in a hundred rivers
their shoot-white palms,
their violet faces,
drifting like great bouquets
or leis tossed on the waves
in offering.

For lovers on piers and bridges
the moon is a gardenia
in a dark bowl,
but something else rides
the shining water,
thumps the pilings
like an exhausted swimmer:
a token of love, such blossoming!

# Foul Play

The man who drives the boarding tunnel
at the airport dreams only of home.
When he eats his cottage cheese at lunch
it is nothing like sturgeon eggs;
he doesn't care a thread about the Baltic.

He says the space between the yellow lines
is room enough, that he will leave
oceans and mountains and gin
at 20,000 feet for the adventurous.

His wife waits each afternoon to see
his face come down the walk
with the family dog and the slap
of the evening news.

When they unload his body in Las Vegas,
stiff and huddled over like a blue valise,
it rides the carousel for over three hours
before anybody claims it—his brother,
saying, "I knew it would end like this."

# Your Responsibility

Tonight on the Schnellzug
a man will leave Salzburg
with a block of fragrant cheese for dinner.
By the time he arrives in Vienna
his whole compartment will smell
of tilsit or cream havarti,
maybe of something stronger,
a good, ripe bierkase.

He will sit alone, staring out the window,
watching the landscape change
as the mountains fall away,
occasionally studying his own reflection
while the glass turns darker somewhere
between Gmunden and Linz.

In his mind he will make love
to a girl he saw in Salzburg,
his hands on her lovely hips just so.
He may smoke or doze, his mind
racing over a thousand details of the day,
but never once will he think of you,
not once of you or America or
the whole Western Hemisphere.

Instead, it is for you to think of him,
as he opens his package enroute to Vienna
and cuts a thick slice of cheese.

# Diagnosis

On the x-ray he never sees, it shows up
as a dark spot, a carbon smudge on paper.
The doctor describes it to him as a dime-
sized growth at the base of the brain,
to put it in proportion and layman's terms,
to make him think of it as small change.
He begins to imagine it, to feel it
like a coin in his pocket, a prized amulet
polished and carried for luck.

Soon, he starts taking chances, driving his car
on the frozen Missouri, out where the ice
groans like old boards and the dull fish
settle deeper into mud; passing
on hillsides and blind curves, sometimes
driving for miles in the oncoming lane
far out in the country with no headlights,
the needle pointing 80 on the darkened dial.

In his dreams he is always swimming out
beyond the channel markers, where the black waters
chop and roll, where seaweed floats
beneath his feet, brushing the fine hairs on his legs.
He avoids the lights of boats; hugging the curved
horizon, he rides the seam between sea and sky,
kicking and pulling himself beyond exhaustion,
deeper into the dark spot on his brain,
feeling like the luckiest man alive.

# Elegy for a Writer in Residence

He was a man mad for meaning,
keen for hidden messages,
burning with the pure desire for
signals in the night sky,
signs among the table scraps,
the rat in the wall
tapping out a clear code.
Sometimes he talked
to his coat in the closet
where even on the hook it
held something of his shape.
One morning we found him
prodding his excrement like
a smuggler looking for diamonds.
So much we did not understand:
how his rich blood murmured
in his ear, how sometimes alone
he wept for no reason at all,
how the mildew in the shower
seemed to spell his name.

## Writer's Block

Just when the man with the pince-nez
says nothing worse could possibly happen,
in strides Granger smelling like Oklahoma.

He ignores the gasp that goes up from
the few guests who haven't already left
and makes his way straight to a tray
of finger sandwiches.

By now the room is completely empty,
except for Granger and the poet he confronts,
saying, "Want to make something of it?"
The answer "Yes" is bound to be misunderstood.

# Edges

She asks me to sharpen her knives, dull
since her husband died, their rough
blades dragging through carrots, butchering
tomatoes on the bright formica.

She wants an edge so keen its cut will leave
her breathless, the lightest stroke splitting
the tight grains of potatoes, sliding
through the gristle of tough pot roasts.

She knows too well how the blunt
edge separates, shredding the delicate fibers,
sawing away like a dull ache
at the onion skin, the thin breast bone.

She thinks the gray whetstone can change
her life, scraping knife after knife so sharp
it shaves the fine hairs on her wrist
and frees the coarse thread
wound into a knot below her heart.

# The Washday Ascension

Across the city women are rising
with their laundry, lifted
sheet by towel by tablecloth
into blues beyond Monday.
One by one they ascend
with pillow slips
or swing from the sleeves
of blue work shirts.
Such a colorful flock,
maneuvering the sky, catching
thermals from chimneys and parking lots,
all morning they drift above
the unsuspecting town, a nosegay of balloons,
a regatta of kites.

When sons and husbands return
from another day of heaviness, dropping
boots on the kitchen floor like weights,
everything is ironed and folded
or hanging on its hook.
And when they fall asleep at night,
hungry for wind and wings,
for that highest stretch of sky,
the last and palest blue before blackness,
the sheets stretched and tucked in tight
beneath them do not rise;
they do not even flutter.

## After the Flood

Half the pictures floated off the walls
and disappeared, except the few
seined in the kitchen screen—
Grandma and Uncle Robert and a group
of unnameable cousins limp as guppies.

The carpeting, so rich with silt
you said we could plant potatoes,
had to be carried out in sections,
along with the dripping mattress
bloated like an ocean sponge.

Each closet we opened was a drained
aquarium, thick with exotic fish.
Everything had to be thrown out—
shelves of drowned books,
even the plants bobbing in their pots.

Now, from the basement you call my name,
laughing, splashing in a dark pool
like a child or a dolphin,
coaxing me down the dangerous stairs,
saying it's time to begin.

## Jigsaw Lovers

*(for Bob Hoover)*

Taking shape on the kitchen table
is a crazed landscape, its cracked hill
piled above the lake
and what will likely be
two people in a boat paying
no attention at all to the gapped sky.
Her half-smile says they are in love,
and their hands, when found,
will no doubt be together.
They depend on one another,
though his face, just discovered,
is turned away and half in shadow
as if he has a secret
or some dark thing to tell her.
They may after all be separate,
her folded hands alone and in her lap,
his on the oars or buried in his pockets.
Around them the jumbled world takes shape,
a piece at a time, locking them in place,
as they float on the finished lake and wait.

## Motherload

Every letter is a boxcar of chipped granite,
little pieces adding up to unliftable weight
that somehow the postman manages
to hoist into the mailbox once a week.

I drag each one into the house, imagining
you, Mother, walking your freight to the corner drop
an inch at a time, the way delivery men
move washing machines and frost-free refrigerators.

The one that arrived today tapped the metal box
no louder than a moth and lies now on the table
looking thin, light as a communion wafer,
but I can't bring myself to open it

because I know it will say you can't go on this way,
and I know I will agree.

## The Sentry

When she cut down the hedge
(tall enough for a man to crouch behind),
we said we understood how a woman
alone needed to feel secure.
Next went the maple sapling, felled
with the same dull ax because
it blocked her view of the street,
and we imagined her squared on the lawn,
never hitting the same place twice,
the young tree shuddering.
In the spring she pulled weeds
and flowers alike, letting nothing
grow beside the house, and tore
the rose from the backyard fence,
coiling its vine like barbed wire
in her gloved hands. Sumac and honeysuckle
and anything that spread or grew back
fast, she poisoned with gasoline.
When she finished, the house
loomed over its barren lot
stark as a stone or pillar of salt,
a private cell, a lookout peak
with a commanding view.

## Saying

They say,
"If you plant potatoes at the proper time,
by the dark of a new moon,
you'll have a successful crop,"
as if potatoes knew
the different phases of the moon—
something like the ocean, maybe,
feeling the soft tug of distance.

My father believes;
his faith exceeds mine.
So we're here in the garden,
digging dark furrows in the night.
The soil smells familiar,
like the expected odor of a relative's house.
Each spadeful brings up a memory
of something half-forgotten.

Above our heads, the dark moon climbs
a dark sky bright with stars,
as we work without speaking,
thinking of sleep, of the deep night,
of how we live off what is buried.

## Inheritance

When my father died he left behind
new shoes, larger than his normal size,
a better fit for my foot than for his.
My mother saved them when she packed
his clothes in boxes for the needy and gave
them to me along with the pocket knife
he always carried and his wallet
bulging with photographs.

I keep these memories safe,
the knife and wallet hidden
beneath my socks in the bureau drawer,
the shoes, with the print of his toes
still on the insole, preserved
in a box in the basement.
His old clothes turn up everywhere:
in line at the grocery store,
sitting on a strange front porch,
bent over the hood of a car stalled in traffic.
Now and then one of his hats comes down the street,
cocked almost the way he wore it,
shading the eyes of some old man who shoulders
past me without speaking, without looking back.

## Farmer

One hail storm changed his life.
The bright ice blew into the field like shrapnel,
exploding over the roof in the dark of a deep sleep.
When my mother woke she found him crouched
among the beaten plants like a child shooting marbles,
a shaman in the desert divining signs, about to tell
the future.

> What jewels, what sweet green
> crushed and floating on the air!
> The wind rushing that way
> into maples and box elders;
> the moon, the sky, the ragged moon!

God and a doctor sent him to Detroit
to turn four screws on an endless line of doors,
to stand awkward and alone amid strangers and fields
of metal. When he slept at night the plant roared
in his ears, like rain, like hail in thick oaks,
sweeping down the yard, crossing the broad-leafed fields,
changing everything.

> Who was that man in his dream
> sitting cross-legged in the mud?
> What was he saying
> when his face loomed up at work, floating
> above the long line of parts?
> Was it rain or tears?
> A sob or mud sucking at a shoe?

After two years he moved us back to Tennessee
and took a job filling vending machines. He never
farmed again. What he saw that night in the chilled
air at Hickory Point remained his secret.
But I remember him every night of his life
standing in the long shadows of our back yard,
himself barely more than a shadow on the black grass,
watching the sky for weather.

## My Father's Best Picture

My mother and brother and I stand
perfectly still, holding our breath
and everything for the shutter.
Our smiles say it is all right
to wear 1950's styles forever
on this black and white lawn
where the bird never sings
or flies from his tree.
We are looking at my father
as he slowly frames and focuses.

If you could look deep into our eyes
you would see him reflected there,
his head bowed over the black box camera,
trying hard to get it right.

Look deeper and you'll see him laugh,
taking another step backward,
almost trampling the brilliant irises.
The wind that makes his cheeks blush
blows his tie across his shoulder
like a blue scarf, rocks
the limbs of the budding maple.
From somewhere a chickadee calls.

On his side the world is all
sound and color; everything's in motion,
and he keeps saying over and over again
that we should "Hold it" "Hold it"
as he moves across the lawn
making infinite adjustments,
saved forever from our small extinction.

# The Passenger

A glider comes in low
beneath the heavy overcast
and circles the small clearing
where I stand waving both arms.
Through the canopy I can see
my father's face and another
I do not recognize looking down.
The wind is the only sound,
rushing past the wings, through
the thick cedars on every side.
He looks unafraid,
my father who never flew;
he looks almost brave,
floating there beyond my reach
and the sound of my voice
calling Father.

Suddenly, the plane begins to climb,
lifted by unseen thermals, rising
higher until it vanishes
into the solid sky.

For a long time I study the after-image
in my eyes, but that fades, too,
leaving only a gray expanse,
leaving a man without a father
who will never be a father,
speaking a child's first word
over and over again.

II

## Baking

I have tried
to keep my hands off your thick pies—
deep-dish and running with juices
of apples and cinnamon
enough to drive a man to voyages,
sailing the ponderous blue for spice—
your delicate cakes,
light with beaten egg whites
and fragrant with anise or almond.

In the oven now, something heavy,
laced with brandy and a pinch of mace,
makes the whole room swoon, rising,
mixing the air with flour and cream
and something else which, lacking
the ingredient, we call love.

## Caring for Succulents

Water them too much and they wither,
weakening like pasta, curling in upon themselves,
a drowned man's bloodless fingers.
Water them too little and they turn
brittle, as dry as matzo, with an edge
that can crumble or cut like paper.

Too much light and they blemish,
flecked or completely burnished
the color of old coins;
not enough and they grow blanched,
a spindly child with anemia or worms.

Sometimes, even when water and light
are in the right proportion, one may become
rootbound, sending out blooms or runners
like a bored husband,
telling you to change its life.

# Naming the Icebergs

On a calm day they may
float by, a fleet of bright sails
so easy to avoid we laugh
at the odd regatta,
giving each cold ship a name.

But in a storm they can pitch
and roll past, crashing
through the water like freighters,
their thick hulls low,
anonymous.

Just last night we had
a narrow miss, feeling
the air chill suddenly,
the jolt as the keel
grazed something submerged.

Saying nothing afterwards,
we sat gripping the rail,
as though silence would steer,
through all our unnamed darknesses,
a course less blind, more true.

# Breakage

This morning I broke the bud vase
on your dresser, the one with the delicate glaze,
your favorite for small bouquets
of violets or a sprig of honeysuckle.

All day I've been trying to glue it back together,
hunched over the parts on the kitchen table
like a man divining bones or entrails,
knowing the bird will never fly again.

Two pieces identical in size and shape
suggest a chance encounter or some shocking
revelation; one sliver, needle-sharp,
points north and stands for grief.

Any moment now, you will come through that door
to find me sitting here before this augury,
my face revealing plainly that I see
something more in this than accident.

# Museo del Oro, Bogotá

Dark rum glows in the glass
like impure gold
and the leaden mood goes on.
It has followed us
all the way from the Museo
and now weights down the table
where we sit drinking, hoping
this drink or the next will change
at least the way we see.

Tonight the guard will lock himself
inside a tomb of gold,
becoming for a while a living pharoah,
knowing in the morning he can take
nothing with him to his other life
of corrugated tin and split linoleum.

Later, when you fumble for the switch
and we stand looking at the gray drapes,
the single bed in our small room,
we close our eyes against the glare,
remembering the guide
who made us wait in a darkened vault,
then turned on all the lights at once
to blind us with gold on every side,
his bright illusion.

# The One

*(for Nancy, Christmas 1979)*

This year we cut our tree in the rain,
slogged through the weeds and muddy fields
to look at an assortment
of dripping cedars, walked round and round
them as though buying livestock or cars,
commented on bald spots and double trunks,
shook our heads at height and breadth like experts.
I kept splashing off through drizzle and puddles
toward some distant shape that always proved to be
split or brown or one-sided, as you waited patiently
for me to jog back, shaking my head, giving
the bad appraisal. We finally took one
you picked with an eye for its potential.

Now I know you were right; it looks good in our window,
hung with glass balls, tinsel, and lights.
And I am beginning to see how in that whole drenched field,
standing alone on the hillside beneath your umbrella,
you were the one I returned to, again and again.

## Rehearsal Dinner

After the plates have been cleared
and the last guest lingers in the doorway,
the man who will be my father-in-law
this time tomorrow pulls me aside
and points to a stain on the starched tablecloth,
the spot where the big roast stood, saying,
"Tell me what you see."
I see an oval of grease turning the linen
translucent, showing the dark wood underneath.
He sees a fish, a perfect fish,
and he smiles as he follows its outline
with his finger, making me see it, too.

This is the photo no one took, not found
among the others in the album: two men bent
over a table, divining a sign
soon to be bleached out, each waiting
for the other to glow with revelations.

I know now we should not have given up;
we should have gone to the kitchen
and laid out rows of streaked plates,
bowls smeared with meaning,
cups stained with the tint of true vision.
We should have dropped to our knees on the linoleum
and read between the tines of forks,
along the broad blades of knives and the arched spoons,
looked deep into pots, through glasses
clouded by fingerprints and melting ice.

Instead, we turned and walked toward sleep,
dreaming our separate dreams of fish swimming
a surf so white we thought no one would believe it.

# The Truth About the Universe

*(for Nancy)*

She palms the orange and turns it,
as serious as a jeweler looking for flaws.
(Hers is the only true gravity,
she the central star
to be encircled forever
and worshiped by primitive hearts.)
With a thumbnail she takes the orange apart,
first the skin, filling the air with bittersweet,
then the white pulp, the veins that cling.
She separates the segments,
laying them on her plate like sculpture,
two rows of small crescents,
delicate moons curling into themselves.

Across the room, I have begun to chant
something dark and aboriginal,
singing passion and the blood,
knowing all I'll ever know of love, of pure desire,
each time she lifts a portion to her lips,
each time the bright fruit bursts
like a sun in the bell of her mouth.

## Snow Ordinance

All the men are out early, surveying
lines between the ends of their cars
and where they know the street should be,
looking for their driveways and sidewalks.
All would make bad farmers, veering off
the row a dozen times, plowing into the dead
lawn, leaving ragged furrows.
Luckily, there will be no evidence, no
wild corn in August or soybeans tangled,
only the straight slab
rasping now beneath their shovels.

If a neighbor leaves for work without
shoveling, gunning his car down the packed
drive, sliding into the street, they pause
long enough to return his wave, cursing
him all the while, the one disordered
life that turns a whole block of exact snow
into an arctic waste.

## Classified

"Free to first caller,
a complete set of *National Geographic*
from August 1968 until last month,
when I let my subscription lapse."

They kept sending me notices,
but I just couldn't take it anymore;
my house doesn't have enough corners,
and issues kept piling up everywhere.
Most of Scandinavia
occupies a straightback chair in the bedroom;
the rivers of Europe flood the hall;
tigers crouch behind the sofa;
tropical birds preen on the credenza;
and the natives are restless under the coffee table.
This morning, before I could fix breakfast,
I had to move the Australian Outback
and Carnival in Rio into another room.
Things have become that desperate.

Won't someone out there call,
anytime after 5 P.M., and volunteer
to take this vast world off my hands?

# At the Railroad Crossing: A Practical Guide

You can play the radio if you're alone,
read a good swatch of a novel
(assuming you have a book on hand),
or stare straight ahead at nothing
in particular. Some people find it helpful
to fantasize about power or sex,
though this brings its own frustrations
and in some cases makes matters worse.
A man from Iowa City claims
to masturbate each time he's stopped,
as many as six times a day during
grain season, but his technique
is clearly not useful to everyone.

At no time should you try to count
the cars or read the gross volume figures
on the grain hoppers. This activity
may increase your agitation or produce
partial disorientation, a kind of
rapture of the rails.
Best to relax; take it like a long
drought or a dull oration which has
to end finally, the last car clapping
past like rain or grateful applause.
The railroads sympathize;
and once in a great while, to ease your boredom,
they make you a present of a blue caboose.

## Endings

Already, I am looking
for a way to end this poem,
if not the click of a box,
then the sound of a dime
dropped on tile, rolling
toward a distant wall.

Beginnings take care of themselves:
wars break out; fires leap up in houses;
diseases spread like tea spilled
on fine linen; lovers, without trying,
fall in love.

Somewhere, a man working alone
turns a copper pipe a thread too far;
water is filling his basement.
Everything depends on how he stops it.

# The Haunting

Today I left my watch
lying on the bureau
where it spent the morning
clucking to itself,
brooding another noon, another sunset,
another darkening sky.
Determined not to be late
I was early everywhere and soon
found myself half-a-day ahead,
living my own future.

When I came in at one
to find you eating alone
your sandwich and shining peach
you looked at me as at a stranger
and somewhere in the rushing chamber
asked, in a voice too small to be
your own, if anything was wrong.

There was a prophecy in all of this:
you expecting no one, familiar
as a widow with your lonely lunch,
and I arriving spectral in the room,
with nothing to say
and nothing but time on my hands.

## Waking as if from Sleep

The sun is shining like a nearer star,
and what few clouds there are look like
wisps of moisture hung above the trees.
My neighbor, fortified with coffee,
comes out of his house and drives away
just like a man going to work.
Already, the street is as hot as asphalt,
and the heat rising from it wavers
in the air like heat.
How much longer I can sit here
stirring this congealed egg, yellow
as a yolk, before this window
blank as glass, is anybody's guess.
Sooner or later I must get up
and face this day I don't want to face,
like the man I know I am, facing it.

III

## Clearing the Field

We begin in waist-high weeds,
spiked nettle and jimson,
wading out as if in water,
hands floating above the green crests,
feet feeling for the bottom.

All day we recover limbs
and stones sunk in the deep field,
dragging each to a central pile,
the two of us straining under
the weight of irregular rocks,
pulling hard to free branches
from the undergrowth of grass and vines
where they lie tangled like wreckage.

Before darkness our salvage
will stand taller than the weeds,
a mound heaped, above land made ready
for the hay mower, the plow,
the even rows of corn,
rising from the immaculate field,
a dark and secret ruin.

# Hunter's Moon

They are out tonight
harvesting the full light in the field,
their faces stern with death,
almost phosphorescent.

They could have risen from the field itself,
a colony of strange mushrooms, deadly,
spreading over moonlit ground.

In the distance they are sleepwalkers,
lugging the dead weight of their bodies,
pulling against the black soil.

Toward morning they return
to mothers and wives who pulled shades
against the brilliant night
and lay alone with life,
curled beneath the covers as though wounded.

## Killing Weather

My neighbor is slaughtering hogs.
Across the field I can hear
his rifle snap on the crisp air,
faint as a single hand clap,
once . . . twice . . . three times,
a slow applause.
He has waited weeks
for a morning cool enough,
watching the fields for frost,
looking for thin ice in the weeds
at the edge of the pond,
for a single drop of water
frozen on the well pump.
Now he stands in the pen
like a marksman,
hearing the shrill squeals,
feeling the brass shells
turn colder in his pocket.

Soon his shed will be hung
with hams and shoulders,
with sides of salted pork
and slabs of bacon.
Soon, too, his wife
will shiver in the kitchen,
pulling her housecoat close
about her while the thick meat
sputters in a pan.
Outside, the fields will fill
with snow; the pond will freeze
as hard as marble;
and the well pump will turn so cold
no one can touch it with his naked hand.

## The Sacrifice

The deer rise up in the fields
by the highway and hurl themselves
into the hard bodies of cars.

They come into town
from the far hills and leap
through department store windows.

They stand perfectly still
among willows, listening
for the sound of the killing shot.

When the hunter kneels over a fallen buck
he counts the points in his rack,
again and again, like a rosary.

# Tracker

*(for Dick Wright)*

The prints you find in new snow by your door
are ones you know well: raccoon and sparrow and fox squirrel.
Even the heavy scarf wrapped twice around your face
cannot hide your disappointment.
You had hoped for something else, some strange spoor
to follow down the frozen fields.

To make you happy,
I would carve a claw of pine and cork
to leave a track no one has ever seen.
But you would follow the path too well,
back through stubbled corn and the dead grove
to the place by the road where I would
put on my boots again.

You have seen false trails before,
following each into the tangled
trees and briars to disclose the source of the lie.
Now, the game tires you,
and each evening you sit alone at your window,
tracing the arc of the known moon
through fields of familiar stars.

## To My Unborn Children

Son, you will wait forever in a private place,
floating on brackish backwater
in a cave that smells of fish.
You, too, daughter, will lie quietly there,
a bright shell drowned in darkness.
Whatever tides there are will not reach you;
no current will pull you from your sleep.
When the gull swings wide in the wind
above the surf, her shrill voice keening,
you will not hear or know she cries for you.

If you were strong swimmers
parting the waves with your hands
or forms on the beach with familiar faces
lifted in the sun,
I could not love you better.
You are with me always,
deep in your dark perfection.

# The Young Man Writes of Death

*(for Marvin Bell)*

Each year he moves a little closer
to the coast, starting out in Kansas,
in a lake of wheat, old farmers
mocking his awkward paddle,
whooping out loud at his serious dives.
This time next year he will be
the object of fun in the Ozark Range,
awed at the edge of some ravine,
atop some sloping hill where mountain
men laugh and lift clear jars,
dealing with height and depth their own way.
By the time he reaches the Mississippi,
he will have learned to laugh himself,
skimming a few flat stones across the current,
and later, when he swears he's seen a gull
circling a cornfield in Illinois, too far inland
to be believed, someone will believe him,
may even ask him home for dinner.

# To My Left Hand

Poor illiterate,
cramped in silence like a claw
or tapping on the table top
in meaningless code,
a message even you don't understand,
except to say you're empty,
wanting to grasp something,
unschooled and unsure,
fumbling with buttons and hooks,
gauche before silverware,
clumsy with teacups,
brooding with lint in a sinister pocket.
By day your adroit friend
flips coins, doodles, balances liquids,
makes the most eloquent gestures
as you hang limp and dumb
or flutter nearby, an afterthought,
never the first to reach out,
inverted twin in a world forever backward.
At night, sometimes I wake
to find the two of you clutching one another
like jealous brothers,
like old men weeping or strangers
afraid of identical dark.

# Sketching Audubon

*Audubon had tasted and sampled all the birds he
killed; and reported that he found flickers
disagreeable because they fed on ants, herring gulls
too salty, but starlings delicate.*

 —Lewis Mumford, The Pentagon of Power


My brush makes everything whole again,
healing shattered beaks and torn wings,
hiding the blood congealed in fine down
like a thick sauce.

Those small birds plucked and roasting
on the spit will once again perch
on the arched stem of a wild rose,
so real you can almost hear them singing.

They sing to me now, turning brown
in the licking flames, filling the air
with their aroma clearer and more true
than any note.

In years to come I will look at them
sketched in this book or framed
and hanging on a wall, and I will recall
this night, the moon drifting like a feather,
and the taste of their sweet, dark flesh.

# What Dying Must Be Like

Imagine a man beneath a sky
the color of crankcase oil, waiting
with an empty suitcase on a black corner
for a bus that never comes.

After a while he stops fidgeting,
stands perfectly still,
his eyes two brilliant stones: obsidian.

# Pallbearers

*(in memory of Addie Bowers)*

My brother lifts from the other side,
surprised as I am by the weight,
squaring his feet for balance
in the loose gravel of the drive.
She failed so toward the end,
her body withering, that we expected
a husk, a molted skin, but not
this dead stone weight.
Now eight of us, all grandsons,
lean into the load, walking
carefully over uneven ground
toward the hole draped with tarpaulin.
From graveside, the preacher speaks
while we stand looking off into woods
at redbud, at dogwood blossoms opened
just this morning, feeling the certainty
of her passing, not in his words
but in our backs and along
the tightened muscles of our arms.

# Lovely to Think So

*(in memory of D.C.)*

The day he died, fish rose
all over the city, floating up
from flooded gutters into brighter,
lighter atmospheres, sailing
with the wind like Chinese kites.
The Safeway butcher threw out
a box of prime beef by mistake
and twelve dogs ate well
in the shadow of the loading dock.
Later in the week, all the teams
in little league wore black bands
on their caps and tried to hit
one into the brush for old times' sake.
An old man rose from the bus stop
bench as the hearse passed by,
rubbing his lower back
exactly where a tail might be,
smiling all the while at the thought.

# Notes

*(for Helen)*

One in the bathroom
reminds her to take her pills;
another on the kitchen cabinet
lists items needed from the store—
flour, corn starch, a box of salt—
things that are hard to remember.
Her calendar is covered with tiny messages,
so many diagonal words
angled through the boxes of dates
the numbers themselves are hard to see—
check-ups, birthdays, reminders to pay bills.

Alone in the house with her memory failing
she carries on this piecemeal correspondence
with herself, leaving words of advice
and kind reminders everywhere
like a lover or a faithful friend.
Sometimes when she finds a note misplaced
weeks before, she reads it over and over
as if it were a poem or a rare manuscript.

Each night, before she turns out the light,
she takes one last piece of paper and tapes it
to the skin beneath her gown,
exactly between her withered breasts.
It is addressed to the ambulance men and says,
"I have a bad heart. Revive me.
Please revive me. I need oxygen."

# Forty

*(for Loring)*

We are hiding in your living room,
fifteen of us holding our breath
like one large organism, waiting
to spring forward when you enter,
wanting to see your face
that instant before composure
when you realize your best friends
can betray you.
It is the classic look we're after,
a mix of puzzlement and pleasure
tinged with pain, the look of Caesar
when he feels the cold steel
in the friendly palm.
We carry, each of us, unsheathed
and glinting with our smiles,
the cutting edge we've honed
for weeks in privacy—
the bright remark, the unsubtle stab
of a joke about growing old.
On this day you've waited for and feared,
we've gathered here in dark conspiracy,
to see how well you bear the wound.

## Making It Last

I cut my roses on the bias
and drop an aspirin in the vase
to help them hold their heavy heads
a little longer, a trick
my mother taught me
who also knew how to keep meat
in summer, apples in winter,
and could make the best use of any chicken
feathers for pillows, bones for broth,
bloody water for the flower beds.

If she were alive
she would smile approvingly
to see me storing honey upside-down,
unwrapping bars of soap
to let them harden in the air,
pulling the drapes
against the morning light
to keep the rug from fading.
I forget whether the slipcover
on the sofa was her idea or mine.

Since I never let the cat outside
he is free from the usual dangers
and may live another dozen years,
may even outlive me.
He watches through the screen
as I plant a garden of things
to can or freeze: tomatoes,
bush beans, crookneck squash.
In the winter he lies nearby
as I savor this food
before a southern window,
making the most of a diminished sun.

# The Secret

*(for Linda)*

Somewhere in the mountains,
in the thick shade of blue spruce and pine,
is a horse that will come to no one but you.
Others have called him, but you alone
know his name, saying it softly
in your sleep like a sigh or a rosary.

Each night he stands just outside your window,
nuzzling the wet grass on the lawn.
Each day he waits in shadows,
in the flat light among saplings.
He is always there, more faithful than a lover,
waiting for you to call his name.

# Driving without Lights

At first we thought it was fog or heavy overcast,
but the beams grew weaker by the moment, shrinking
to a yellow haze on the road just beyond our bumper,
making every foot of pavement a revelation.

Afraid to stop, we slowed our speed and traveled on,
continually entering the dim mouth of a cave,
not knowing what passageways or caverns lay beyond.

When someone passed us, swinging his bright lights
through our windows, we vowed to follow
no matter the turns he took, but he drove too fast,
his taillights vanishing beyond some unseen hill,
leaving us weaving from ditch to ditch.

Slowly, we trained our eyes to see, straining into darkness,
discovering not only the road again, but the owl perched
in his oak, the doe lifting her head in milkweed
by the field's edge, the wide-eyed little ones, discovering
also some small part of ourselves in love with darkness,
not afraid to gather speed along this long, black highway.

# THE MINNESOTA VOICES PROJECT

*1981*

\# 1 Deborah Keenan, HOUSEHOLD WOUNDS (poems), $3.00

\# 2 John Minczeski, THE RECONSTRUCTION OF LIGHT (poems), $3.00

*The First Annual Competition*

\# 3 John Solensten, THE HERON DANCER (stories), $5.00

\# 4 Madelon Sprengnether Gohlke, THE NORMAL HEART (poems), $3.00

\# 5 Ruth Roston, I LIVE IN THE WATCHMAKERS' TOWN (poems), $3.00

\# 6 Laurie Taylor, CHANGING THE PAST (poems), $3.00

*1982*

\# 7 Alvaro Cardona-Hine, WHEN I WAS A FATHER (a poetic memoir), $4.00

*The Second Annual Competition*

\# 8 Richard Broderick, NIGHT SALE (stories), $5.00

\# 9 Katherine Carlson, CASUALTIES (stories), $5.00

\#10 Sharon Chmielarz, DIFFERENT ARRANGEMENTS (poems), $3.00

\#11 Yvette Nelson, WE'LL COME WHEN IT RAINS (poems), $3.00

*1983*

\#12 Madelon Sprengnether, RIVERS, STORIES, HOUSES, DREAMS (familiar essays), $4.00

\#13 Wendy Parrish, BLENHEIM PALACE (poems), $3.00

*The Third Annual Competition*

#14  Perry Glasser, SUSPICIOUS ORIGINS (short stories), $6.00

#15  Marisha Chamberlain, POWERS (poems), $3.50

#16  Michael Moos, MORNING WINDOWS (poems), $3.50

#17  Mark Vinz, THE WEIRD KID (prose poems), $3.50

#18  Neal Bowers, THE GOLF BALL DIVER (poems), $3.50

*Copies of any or all of these books may be purchased directly from the publisher by filling out the coupon below and mailing it, together with a check for the correct amount and $1.00 per order for postage and handling, to:*

New Rivers Press
1602 Selby Ave.
St. Paul, MN 55104

_____

Please send me the following books: _____

_____

_____

_____

_____

_____

I am enclosing $ _____ (which includes $1.00 for postage and handling) Please send these books as soon as possible to:

NAME _____

ADDRESS _____

CITY & STATE _____

ZIP _____